The Wisdom of

Vernon Coleman and Donna Antoinette Coleman

Published by Blue Books

First published by Blue Books in 2012 in a limited edition.

This book is copyright. Enquiries should be addressed to the author c/o the publishers.

Copyright Vernon Coleman and Donna Antoinette Coleman 2014

The right of Vernon Coleman and Donna Antoinette Coleman to be identified as the authors of this work has been asserted in accordance with the Copyright, Designs and Patents Act 1988.

Contents List

Prologue 1
Chapter 1 Animals Can Communicate With One Another (And With Us) 7
Chapter 2 Animals Can Treat Themselves When They Are Ill 9
Chapter 3 Animals Protect Themselves From Insects 22
Chapter 4 Animals Are Capable Of Love 24
Chapter 5 Animals Are Sentient Creatures 28
Chapter 6 Animals As Teachers 29
Chapter 7 Animals As Carers: How Animals Help People 30
Chapter 8 Animals Can Use Tools 35
Chapter 9 Animals Eat The Foods They Need 38
Chapter 10 Animals Have Feelings 41
Chapter 11 Animals Have Powerful Homing Instincts 42
Chapter 12 Animals Have Powerful Imaginations 44
Chapter 13 Animals Enjoy Playing 45
Chapter 14 Why Animals Hide Their Pain To Protect Themselves 47
Chapter 15 Animals Have Their Own Pets 48
Chapter 16 Animals Can Be Self-Conscious 49
Chapter 17 Animals Can Be Artistic 50
Chapter 18 Animals Have Good Memories 51
Chapter 19 Animals Give One Another Presents 53
Chapter 20 Animals Have Much Better Survival Instincts Than We Do 54
Chapter 21 Animals Exhibit Altruistic Behaviour 56
Epilogue What We Can Learn From Animals 60

Appendix 1 Facts About Animal Experiments 61
Appendix 2 Reasons For Being A Vegetarian 64

Dedicated

To Ed Lee, our friend, and a true friend to the animals

Prologue

It's surprisingly difficult to obtain real facts about animals. Much of what we read, and think we know, owes more to imagination than to science. Rumour, gossip and folklore have, over the years, taken the place of solid research. Surprisingly little accurate research has ever been done into the way animals live and behave.

In the case of wild animals this is not, perhaps, too surprising. Studying wild animals properly means following them for years in their natural habitat - a difficult if not impossible task which requires superhuman dedication and would, in the end, probably produce research of questionable value because the very presence of the human observer might well alter the behaviour of the animals. Studying `wild' animals in the entirely unnatural conditions of the laboratory, zoo or safari park is as likely to provide useful information about the way animals behave naturally as studying prisoners would about human behaviour. One thing we do know for certain is that wild animals kept in captivity behave very differently to wild animals living in their natural habitat.

It should, of course, be much easier to observe farm animals. Cows, pigs, sheep and other animals are easy enough to watch. And since the observer need not alter the animals' routine the observations should be of value. But very few proper studies have been carried out on farm animals, and vets and farmers are invariably quite mistaken in their beliefs about animals such as sheep and cows. Instead of watching these animals in their natural surroundings, men and women in white coats cage them, stick electrodes into their heads, sit them in metal boxes for weeks at a time to make them depressed, separate them from their families, sew up their eyes and inject chemicals into their brains while they are awake. The knowledge obtained in such a barbaric way is never of any value but is simply added to our ever-growing library of pointless `discoveries' and `observations'. In a generation or so our descendants will look back at the meat traders, the animal transporters, the hunters and the vivisectors and wonder not just at the sort of people they were, but at the sort of people we were to let them do what they did.

The truth, sadly, is that little or nothing of value has been written or broadcast about pigs, cows, sheep and other farm animals because the meat industry doesn't want us to know that the animals which are reared and killed for us to eat are sensitive, thoughtful and intelligent.

Farmers and butchers have a financial interest in perpetuating and strengthening the myth that animals (particularly farm animals) are stupid. After all, one of the reasons why we don't like to eat horses, dogs or cats is because we recognise that they have intellect and personality. If people knew the truth about the capabilities of pigs, sheep and cows the market for meat would collapse. It is inconvenient to know that sheep are sensitive and intelligent creatures. And so tame academics (a large and malleable group) happily endorse the `farm animals are stupid and so don't matter' myth.

Surprisingly, even many vets are largely ignorant about farm animals. We have, for example, met vets who believed that sheep are colour blind (not true) and that they have only short-term memories of 20 minutes or so (also not true). Most don't realise that sheep hate getting wet. And many mistake their nervousness for stupidity.

Animals possess a wider range of skills than most of us imagine. The one thing humans have that animals don't have is the conceit, the arrogance, to assume we are wiser than all other animals and are, consequently, entitled to do as we will with other members of the animal kingdom.

All animals are special and all are worthy of our awe and respect but, sadly, that respect is the one thing our relationship with animals usually lacks.

Animal abusers will sometimes argue that since human beings can speak foreign languages and do algebraic equations they are inevitably 'better' than animals. What nonsense this is. If we follow this argument to its logical conclusion then we must assume that humans who cannot speak foreign languages or do algebraic equations are in some way second-class and are not entitled to be treated with respect.

Who decides which are the skills deserving of respect?

If we decide that the ability to fly, run at 30 mph, see in the dark or swim under water for long distances are skills worthy of respect there won't be many human beings reaching the qualifying standard.

Cats can find their way home - without map or compass - when abandoned hundreds of miles away in strange territory. How many human beings could do the same?

How many humans could spin a web?

Even seemingly simple animals can think.

Turtles have been observed learning a route from one place to another. To begin with they make lots of mistakes, go down cul de sacs and miss short cuts. But after a while they can reduce their journey time dramatically.

Birds, which might normally be alarmed by the slightest noise, learn to ignore the noise of trains and cars when they build their nests near to railway lines or busy roads.

And oysters are capable of learning too. Oysters which live in the deep sea know that they can open and shut their shells at any time without risk. But oysters which live in a tidal area learn to keep their shells closed when the tide is out - so that they don't dry out and die. This might not quite rank alongside writing a classic novel but how many human beings can write classic novels?

Animals use reason and experience to help them survive and they exhibit all of the skills which the animal abusers like to think of as being exclusively human. For example, animals accumulate information which helps them to survive and live more comfortably. Moreover, they do it just as man does - by discriminating between useful and useless information and by memorising information which is of value. A puppy who has been burnt on a hot stove will keep away from it just as surely as will a child who has suffered a similarly unpleasant experience. Older fish learn to be wary of lures - and become far more difficult to catch than young ones. Rats learn how to avoid traps, and birds learn where telephone wires are strung so that they don't fly into them. Arctic seals used to live on inner ice floes to avoid the polar bears but after man arrived, and proved to be a worse enemy, they started living on the outer ice floes. Many animals know that they can be followed by their scent and act accordingly. A hunted deer or hare will run round in circles, double back on its own tracks, go through water and leap into the air in order to lose its pursuers. Flocks of parrots will send an advance scouting party ahead to check out that all is well.

We owe it to animals to treat them with respect and, at the very least, to leave them alone to live their lives on this earth free from our harm.

Charles Darwin, the author of *On The Origin of Species,* wrote that: `there is no fundamental difference between man and the higher mammals in their mental faculties'. He also argued that: `the senses and intuition, the various emotions and faculties, such as love, memory, attention, curiosity, imitation, reason, etc., of which man boasts, may be found in an incipient, or sometimes even well-developed condition in the `lower' animals.'

The miracles are unending. The honeycomb and the bird's nest are wonders of architecture. Even the seemingly lowly ant has a complex and sophisticated lifestyle. Ants can communicate with one another and recognise their friends. They clean one another, they play, they bury their dead, they store grain, they even clear land, manure it, sow grain and harvest the crop which they have grown. They even build roads and tunnels.

We may not like it but many non-human species have a much greater influence on their environment than we have. There are still tribes of men who live almost naked in very crude huts and whose social structures are relatively primitive when compared to, say, the beavers who cut down trees, transport them long distances, dam rivers, construct substantial homes and dig artificial waterways. Birds build astonishingly beautiful nests from the simplest of materials.

Animals are often curious, determined and hardworking; loving, loyal and faithful. They have many skills we cannot emulate. The eagle and the vulture have eyes as powerful as a telescope. Many animals, birds and insects can predict the coming of storms far more effectively than our allegedly scientific weather forecasters. Weight for weight, the tomtit has more brain capacity than a human being.

Animal behaviour which seems impressive is often dismissed as nothing more than instinctive. But that is patronising and nonsensical. There is now ample evidence available to show animals can invent and adapt tools according to circumstances. That can hardly be called `instinctive' behaviour.

It is truly absurd that when people behave badly they are described as behaving `like animals'. This is a calumny. Animals would never do the terrible things that people do. Animals kill to eat. But they don't kill for vengeance or for pride. They don't kill out of jealousy or spite. They kill for survival and they kill to defend their families. But they don't dress up and go hunting for fun. And they don't start wars. Compared to many human beings animals are civilised, humane, generous and kindly. There is no little irony in the fact that the worst behaving animals are domestic dogs and guard dogs which are trained to attack humans for no reason other than to please their owners.

We have created a hell on this earth for other creatures. Our abuse of animals is the final savagery; the final outrage of mankind in a long history of savagery and outrage. Instead of learning from other animals, instead of attempting to communicate with them, we abuse, torture and kill them. We diminish ourselves in a hundred different ways through our cruelty and our ignorance and our thoughtlessness. 'Man's inhumanity to man makes countless thousands mourn and his inhumanity to not-men makes the planet a ball of pain and terror,' wrote J. Howard Moore.

If man were truly the master of the universe he would use his wisdom and his power to increase the comfort and happiness of all other creatures. But, tragically, man has used his wisdom and his power to increase their misery. Animal abusers imprison millions of animals in cruel and heartbreaking conditions and ignore their cries of pain and distress on the grounds that animals are not 'sentient creatures'. What self-delusional nonsense this is. Sheep and cattle are left out in huge fields in cold, wet weather. They shiver and search in vain for shelter because all the trees and hedgerows have been removed to make the farm more efficient. The animal abusing farmer cares not one jot for animals: he cares only for his profits.

'Until he extends the circle of his compassion to all living things,' wrote Albert Schweizer, 'man will not himself find peace.'

The merciful man is kind to all creatures.

In the pages which follow we have summarised the wisdom of the animals. But be warned: this book may change your life. We believe our book offers clear evidence that animals frequently display the sort of wisdom (and the types of emotion) which many tend wrongly to regard as uniquely human.

Vernon Coleman and Donna Antoinette Coleman, November 2012

Chapter 1   Animals Can Communicate With One Another (And With Us)

Many observers have dismissed the sounds which animals make as simply 'noises', but scientists who have taken the time and trouble to listen carefully to the extraordinary variety of sounds made by different creatures have concluded that animals really can communicate with one another. How arrogant we are to assume that we are the only species capable of communicating and of formulating a formal system of language. It is levelling to realise that animals may, similarly, think that the sounds we make when we talk to one another are no more than pointless noises.

Here are a few examples illustrating the ability of animals to communicate effectively.

1) Scientists studying whales have found that there are patterns of what can only be described as speech in the noises they make.

2) Bees can communicate the direction, distance and value of pollen sources quite a distance away.

3) It is generally assumed that parrots merely repeat words they have heard without understanding what they mean. This is not true. In

their marvellous book *When Elephants Weep* authors Masson and McCarthy report that when psychologist Irene Pepperberg left her parrot at the vet's surgery for an operation the parrot, whose name was Alex, called out: `Come here. I love you. I'm sorry. I want to go back.' Another parrot, in New Jersey, America saved the life of its owner by crying: `Murder! Help! Come quick!' When neighbours ran to the scene they found the parrot's owner lying on the floor, unconscious, bleeding from a gash in his neck. The doctor who treated the man said that without the parrot's cries he would have died. The same parrot woke his owner and neighbours when a fire started in the house next door.

4) Rabbits communicate by thumping on the ground with their hind feet. They can `talk' to one another in this way over distances of 200 yards.

5) Human beings who have taken the time to do so have found that they have been able to communicate well with all other primates.

6) Animals can communicate in ways we haven't really begun to understand. British biologist Rupert Sheldrake conducted an experiment in which he simultaneously recorded humans at work and their dogs at home. The moment the human left work, the dog, waiting at home, headed for the door. This worked even if the human being left work at a different time each day. The daughter of one dog owner reported that their dog always rushed to the door exactly twenty minutes before her mother arrived home. And it didn't matter what time the mother left work. The dog always knew. We are aware of a number of people who have reported similar skills among cats.

7) It is by no means unusual for human beings to receive messages from animals. British author, Sir H. Rider Haggard, once described how he had dreamed that his dog Bob was lying dead in a clump of weeds near some water. In the dream the dog appeared to be telling the author of his forthcoming death. `The next day,' wrote Haggard, `Bob was found dead in just such a place. He had been hit by a train at the same time that I'd had my dream.'

Chapter 2   Animals Can Treat Themselves When They Are Ill

Animals know that there are four main ways to deal with a threatening situation:

a) they can escape from the problem

b) they can remove the problem

c) they can wait for the problem to go away

d) they can search for a solution

These basic responses apply to threats from illness just as much as they apply to threats from predators.

An animal's body, like a human body, can protect, defend and repair itself when under threat. In-built mechanisms enable an animal to exist under quite extraordinarily extreme external conditions. The body's internal mechanisms (some of which are mechanical but most of which are physiological) work readily, speedily and automatically to protect the body from external threats.

Animals recognise the power of what we call 'bodypower'. They know that sometimes not taking medicine is the best way to get well. They understand that fasting, resting, staying warm, allowing vomiting and diarrhoea to do their work, may be the best way. If, however, these systems do not or cannot function, or do not succeed in dealing with the problem, then the animal's instincts and behavioural habits will take over. So, to give a simple example, if the weather is too hot for the internal temperature control mechanisms to defend an animal's integrity, and protect it from damage, then the animal will find some shade or will swim in a pool.

However, if physiological mechanisms and instincts all fail, and the animal falls ill, then the creature will treat itself, using medicaments taken from its surroundings.

Animals don't usually rely on outside doctors, they self-medicate. They use their experience to avoid illness and protect themselves from illness but if they fall ill they treat themselves. Animals may learn from one another – and, if an animal needs help, another will often provide it - but there are no specialist animals working as doctors.

The aim of self-medication is, of course, to re-establish a feeling of well-being. To do that the patient (whether human or animal) needs to have an understanding of his or her own body. He or she needs to know his or her strengths and weaknesses; he or she needs to know what is normal and what is not. And he or she will probably need to change his or her behavioural patterns – often in a quite dramatic way. So, for example, animals will often seek out and consume something they don't normally eat and which has no nutritional benefit.

Naturally, in order to do this, animals need to know where to find the medicaments they may need. And this is where animals excel. Indeed, animals are so good at finding and using natural remedies that many of man's most effective medicinal solutions were identified by observing animals.

In modern orthodox medicine, doctors tend to treat disease by attacking the pathogen alleged to be responsible. Modern, western medicine turns the patient into a battlefield - with the result that in many instances the treatment does more harm than good. The modern doctor tends to ignore the fact that, for example, infections often take hold during stressful conditions and to forget (if they ever knew) that strengthening the human organism is invariably just as important as attacking the disorder. Attacking only the infection or disability means treating only the symptoms rather than the cause.

In contrast, practitioners of traditional Oriental medicine take a more holistic approach, assuming that the pathogen is not the direct cause of the disease, but merely a symptom of an imbalance, a disruption of physiological or psychological homeostasis. Animals favour this philosophy.

The animal approach is a holistic one; treating the whole organism - and attacking any infection - in whatever ways will best produce a positive outcome. Animals understand that when a disease strikes it is often because their organism has in some way been weakened (by, for example, drought, famine or overcrowding) and that if they are to get wholly well again they must tackle internal, as well as external, causes of disease.

It is, of course, only animals living in the wild who are able to treat themselves. Animals on farms, although far more likely to fall ill than animals in the wild, are denied the opportunity to treat themselves by their circumstances. Despite the fact that there is a considerable amount of evidence showing that animals such as cows and sheep are quite capable of diagnosing and treating themselves, farm animals have very limited access to the varieties of natural plants available in the wild.

Farm animals are more likely to fall ill than animals in the wild for several reasons.

First, stocking densities tend to be so high that parasites, for example, spread easily and quickly and become endemic.

Second, animals kept on farms are unlikely to have proper opportunities to exercise. Many, who live indoors, are even denied the health giving properties of sunshine and fresh air. Farm animals may be exempt from the worst excesses of drought and starvation but their lifestyle is far from healthy. Inevitably, the circumstances in which animals are kept mean that psychological problems abound too.

Third, animals are unlikely to be able to enjoy the sort of range of foodstuffs that would be available to them in the wild. The diet farmers give to captive animals bears no relationship to the diet they normally live on. So for example, farmers often give animal waste to vegetarian animals. In the USA, chicken excrement is fed directly to cattle ('to give them protein') and the French Government has admitted illegally feeding human sewage to French cattle. For years, farmers in Britain routinely fed their cattle the ground up brains and spinal cords of other cattle. (It was this that caused the disastrous outbreak of mad cow disease). Farmers ignored the fact that herbivorous ruminants don't eat meat and never engage in cannibalism

In wild, or semi-wild, conditions chickens live in forests in small groups; they scratch around on the forest floor eating worms, insects and pieces of fresh plant. They use the dust and the sun to keep their feathers bright and they bathe when it rains. At night they roost in trees (their claws are adapted for hanging onto branches even while asleep) so that they are safe from predators.

This is a healthy lifestyle for a chicken.

However, this isn't how chickens are kept on most modern farms. Chicken farmers have selectively bred chickens to grow faster and faster. They have doubled the speed at which a chicken matures. Muscle is created before the bird's heart and circulation can cope, and the result is that the birds are constantly ill. Their bones aren't capable of supporting their excess weight and so they get broken bones. They die of thirst and starvation because they cannot reach the automated food and water delivery systems which supply their cages. Eighty per cent of broiler chickens suffer broken bones and 17,000 birds die every day in the United Kingdom because of heart failure. Farmers regard these deaths as an acceptable cost of doing business. The food the chickens are fed is selected according to the cheapest possible formulation and contains just the basic ingredients. (One popular ingredient is ground up dead chicken. They have to do something with all those dead birds.) The chickens are routinely given antibiotics to try to keep them healthy (despite the fact that farmers know that this habit is a major cause of the development of antibiotic-resistant organisms) and they are kept in semi-darkness so that they stay quiet. They suffer from exceptionally high temperatures (especially when the weather is warm), they stand in their own excrement (which is acidic and blisters their feet) and the air they breathe in is full of fumes, bacteria and dust. It is hardly surprising that half of the broiler flocks in the United Kingdom are colonised with bacteria which can cause neurological problems, arthritis, headaches, backache, fever, nausea and diarrhoea in the people who eat them.

Farm chickens, like other farm animals, are given no freedom and no chance at all to self-medicate.

There is also evidence that animals kept in zoos are more likely to fall ill than animals living in the wild. (When animals are born in zoos the keepers usually offer this evidence that the animals must be happy. Would zookeepers also claim that the fact that babies were born in concentration camps was evidence that concentration camp inmates were happy?) Animals in captivity invariably die far younger than they would die if they were allowed to roam free. (At one oceanarium a famous pilot whale was actually thirteen different pilot whales.) Gorillas in captivity are more likely to die of heart disease than gorillas in the wild. Captive elephants and giraffes both develop arthritis and foot problems (disorders which are far less likely to be seen among animals in the wild). Three quarters of the black rhinoceroses in captivity are killed by haemolytic anaemia that doesn't affect black rhinoceroses.

Captive animals show stereotypical movements such as pacing, rocking or weaving. They develop all sorts of unusual habits: rubbing themselves against the bars of their cages or walking backwards and forwards in unsuccessful attempts to soothe their frustrations. Sometimes, captive animals will become angry. For example, elephants are normally the most peaceful of vegetarians but in zoos they occasionally become homicidal.

Stress is a major factor in the development of disease among animals and there is clear evidence that animals in any sort of captivity suffer a great deal of stress. Animals which normally live in the wild do not adapt well when kept in captivity. Their immune systems collapse when they are separated from their families and friends and shut up in cages. Even if wild animals are caught when still young they will often die within weeks or months if they are locked in a cage. Creatures as varied as gorillas and white sharks all tend to fall ill and die if locked up. An animal's immune system is inextricably linked to its surroundings and to its exposure to stress.

There are, of course, other explanations for the poor health animals suffer in captivity. Animals in captivity simply don't have access to the normal variety of foods they might find in the wild (some of which they would undoubtedly use as medicaments). They don't have the same natural grooming opportunities, the same opportunity for exercise, the same variety of companions and the same soils. Because they are in cages or restricted areas they are unable to move away from pathogen hot spots and they may also be unable to develop proper social relationships with other animals of the same species.

Below we have listed examples of some of the ways that animals treat themselves when they are ill. We can learn a great deal by watching how animals deal with disease - particularly infectious disease. Humans have already learned a great deal about medicine and health care by observing animals but we could learn much more

1) Ranchers in Utah used to turn out sick cattle which had diarrhoea, leaving them to fend for themselves. Initially this was done simply to be rid of the ailing animal and to prevent the spread of any disease. The ranchers were, however, surprised when after a few days their cattle repeatedly returned - quite well. An observant rancher followed some sick animals and saw that they travelled to clay banks and fed on the clay until they got better. The clay absorbed the toxins and viruses causing the diarrhoea. Sadly, cattle on modern farms are given little or no opportunity to self-medicate. Animals throughout the world use clay to deal with poisoning - clay detoxifies by binding onto the harmful substances. Humans could probably benefit too and clay pills might save many lives. However, there isn't much profit to be made out of selling clay and so no one is fighting for the right to do so.

2) A worker from the World Wildlife Fund followed a pregnant African elephant for more than a year. During that time the elephant ate a predictable diet, roaming about three miles a day. At the end of her pregnancy the elephant walked more than 15 miles in a single day and headed for a tree of the boraginacea family. Once she had arrived at the tree she ate it. All of it. She ate the leaves, she ate the branches and she ate the trunk. Four days later she gave birth to a healthy calf. Kenyan women brew a tea from the leaves of this tree to induce labour.

3) Chinese herdsmen have seen elderly deer nibbling at the bark and roots of the fleece flower. When the bark and roots were analysed scientists found that they contained ingredients likely to help reduce hypertension, cholesterol levels, coronary heart disease and other disorders common in old age.

4) In the Han Dynasty a defeated general called Ma-Wu and his army retreated to a poor part of China to rest and recover. Many soldiers and horses died. Those left were ill, excreting blood in their urine. One groom noticed that his three horses were healthy, and wisely he watched to see what they ate. He saw that they were eating a good deal of a small plantain plant. So he boiled some of the plant and ate it. The blood quickly disappeared from his urine. He then gave the same plant to the other men and horses. They were all cured. The plant is now known to contain ingredients which make it anti-inflammatory and antimicrobial.

5) In the 17th century, English doctors regarded watching animals as a reputable way of learning about medicines. Queen Anne's personal physician went to the marshes of Essex, where he knew the locals put their sheep when they suffered from a disorder known as 'the rott'. He watched what they ate and by doing so discovered herbs with which he could help human patients with consumption.

6) Native American Indians learnt so much from watching how bears treated themselves when they were ill that advanced healers were known as Bear Medicine Men.

7) A herbalist in Tanzania rescued an orphaned porcupine. When the animal became ill with diarrhoea and bloating the porcupine went into the forest and dug up and ate a plant which turned out to be useful for treating internal parasites in humans.

8) A Creole herbalist in Venezuela watched deer chewing the seed cases of a plant. He subsequently found that the plant helped his human patients.

9) In the Middle Ages, English doctors noticed that when an animal licked its wounds the injury would heal more quickly. The doctors decided that animals' tongues must have some marvellous healing property and so they got into the habit of cutting the tongues out of puppies and using them as wound dressings. This didn't work terribly well and eventually (some centuries later) the doctors realised that it was the saliva which contained both an antiseptic and agents which encouraged wound closure.

10) Domestic cats and dogs chew grass. There are two reasons for this: grass is an emetic (causing regurgitation or vomiting) and a purgative scour (getting rid of worms living further down the intestine). Animals choose different types of grasses for different functions

. 11) Elephants, who are herbivores, need a lot of sodium but there isn't much present in plants. Without the sodium they become ill. So the elephants need to find their sodium elsewhere. In Kenya, there is a series of caves high up on the side of an inactive volcano called Mount Elgon. These caves have been created by generations of elephants. Over the last two million years the elephants have eaten vast quantities of rock. Inside the caves the elephants have to crawl on their knees to dig out lumps of sodium rich rock. They also drink the mineral rich waters which contain calcium and magnesium.

12) When fish find themselves in polluted waters they will swim away as quickly as they can.

13) Gorillas in Rwanda eat rock which they dig out of the slopes of Mount Visoke during the dry season. The rock the gorillas mine and

eat contains a good deal of iron, aluminium and clay. The gorillas eat the rock as a medicine. The clay helps stop diarrhoea (a common problem among gorillas because much of their plant based diet in the dry season causes diarrhoea and dangerous fluid loss) and the aluminium has a useful antacid effect. The iron is useful because in the dry season the gorillas have to go higher to find vegetation and may develop altitude anaemia.

14) Chimpanzees in Tanzania have been seen to eat earth from termite mounds. But they only do this when they are suffering from diarrhoea and other gastrointestinal problems. The termite mounds are rich in clay that helps prevent diarrhoea. Termite mound earth is also used by elephants, giraffes and rhinoceroses.

15) Eating charcoal is an effective way to adsorb toxins. Charcoal is used in human medicine to treat drug overdoses and poisoning and for wind and bloating. We use charcoal because we know that when wild animals find charcoal after forest fires or lightning strikes they will eat the burnt wood even though it doesn't have much nutritional value. Deer and ponies have been seen doing this in the New Forest in England. In Kenya, camels have been seen to eat charcoal. Monkeys have been seen to do it on the island of Zanzibar where their diet includes trees which are high in toxins. The charcoal absorbs these toxins. The monkeys have been seen to consume precisely the amount of charcoal as would be recommended as an effective veterinary dose.

16) When rats are given the poison paraquat they will survive if they find clay to eat to absorb the poison. The rats have to eat the clay for several weeks in order to make sure it carries all the poison out of their bodies. They know this.

17) Civets, colobus monkeys, elephants, bison, pigs, tigers, camels, bears, wild dogs, rhinoceroses, Indian mole rats and jackals are all known to eat plants for their medicinal properties. Toxic plant compounds are sometimes used to control internal parasites.

18) Indian wild bison feed on the bark of horrahena antidysentaria - which is also used to treat dysentery in humans. This plant contains a drug which is active against amoebic dysentery protozoa.

19) Chimpanzees have been observed to eat at least 26 different plant species that are prescribed in traditional human medicine for the treatment of internal parasites. They have been observed to increase their intake of drug rich plants when necessary.

20) Animals sometimes take plants not for their drug action but for mechanical aid. So, for example, chimpanzees suffering with worms have been seen to swallow the leaves of plants which contained nothing which had any effect on parasites. The only thing the leaves had in common was their rough texture and indigestibility. It turned out that the animals were folding up the leaves and then swallowing them. The parasitic worms in the chimpanzees' intestines were being captured by the tiny barbs on the leaves. Folding the leaves increased the chances of the worms being trapped and then excreted.

21) Most wild animals have a low sugar diet and have few problems with tooth decay, but chimpanzees eat a good deal of sugary fruit and suffer from both tooth decay and gum disease. To cope with these two problems they chew on the antibacterial bark of trees. They also inspect and clean one another's teeth. One chimpanzee was seen to prise out the bad teeth of another animal by using a wooden lever she had made.

22) If adult male baboons become wounded (through fighting or hunting) they keep their wounds clean by licking and grooming. Their wounds will also be carefully groomed by female baboons.

23) If chimpanzees who are wounded can reach the area they will lick their wounds. If they cannot reach the injury they will lick their fingers and dab at the wounds. They also dab leaves on a wound, lick the leaves and dab them on the wound again. Infant chimpanzees will lick the wounds of their mothers. The saliva of all mammals is an excellent disinfectant for their own wounds. Domestic dogs lick their wounds because their saliva contains antimicrobials capable of killing bacteria such as staphylococcus,

escherichia coli and streptococcus. Rat saliva contains substances which help speed up the closure of wounds. Human saliva contains healing substances too and it is perhaps possible that we could speed up wound healing by licking our own wounds. Our saliva contains mucins and fibronectins which inactivate microbes by binding them, lactoferrins which kill iron dependent bacteria by taking their iron, peroxidases which poison bacteria, histatin which is a strong antifungal agent and a type of antibody that is active against viruses such as influenza and polio.

24) Stags who are injured in the Neydharting area of Austria will drag themselves miles to immerse themselves and their wounds in the black muddy waters of the moors. The waters and mud have been found to contain over 300 bioactive herbs, many antimicrobials, vitamins and hormones.

25) A capuchin monkey who was badly wounded took a stick, chewed the end to make a brush then used the brush to apply sugary syrup to the wound area (she had been given the syrup as food). A strong sugar solution is a good ointment for wounds. Like honey it has an antibacterial effect

26) Many animals routinely treat their own wounds. Wounded elk, moose, bears and caribou roll in clay. Bears and deer rub themselves on trees which have resin in their bark. Wounded cattle and deer roll in sphagnum moss. Deer living near the sea will walk out into the salty water. Many animals dip wounded areas into cold water to stop bleeding and ease pain. Elephants will cover and pack a wound with mud. In many cases herbalists have found that the substances used (tree bark, mud, etc.) contain antiseptics which will protect the wound and help ensure that it heals.

27) Animals have even been known to make plaster casts. A Pyrenean mountain goat has been seen to make itself a plaster cast using clay, lichen and grass. An injured woodcock took clay from the edge of a stream and smeared it on his leg near the knee. He then pulled up grass roots and put them into the clay. He then added more clay. In the end he had created a very effective clay cast designed to hold his broken leg together. Other natural historians have observed

that snipe which have had a leg broken by a gun shot will bind the injured leg together with their good leg, using feathers to create a cast and then using mud or clay to hold the cast together.

28) Californian ground squirrels will deliberately taunt rattlesnakes so that they are bitten. The ground squirrels are resistant to the venom but the substance stimulates the animals' immune systems and helps slow the spread of cancer and other serious disorders.

29) Fever is a defence mechanism designed to help the body combat infection; a high fever will often kill bacteria. Some animals will take advantage of this phenomenon and deliberately make their temperature rise. So-called cold-blooded animals (e.g. crabs, toads and tortoises) which actively moderate their own temperature will take action to bring on a fever to kill an infection. Lizards who are ill will find somewhere warmer to lie. Fish will move to warmer waters. Ants will bask in the sun if they are ill. If there is a fungus in their hive honeybees will vibrate their wings enough to raise the temperature and prevent larvae being infected. Hedgehogs will sunbathe if they are ill because this helps to push their body temperature higher. (In addition the sunlight acts as an antimicrobial agent).

30) Fasting can help an infected animal get better quicker. Sick animals will (like human beings) stop eating. Bacteria need iron and the body reduces the availability of iron during an infection by not eating.

31) Some animals will deliberately eat plants which boost their immune systems.

32) Bees are very good at fighting infection. They collect resins produced by trees to protect their buds and they make propolis from the resin. They coat the inside of their hive with this, making an environment so sterile it would be the envy of any operating team. The propolis contains hundreds of flavonoids, phenolics and

aromatic compounds. If an invading animal gets into the hive and dies the bees will embalm it by covering it with propolis - to protect against infection. Honey, made as food for winter, is packed with potent antimicrobials to stop it going off. Today, doctors are using honey on human patients. They use it to stimulate the immune system and to treat wounds.

33) Capuchin monkeys rub natural substances such as clematis stems into their fur to repel pests, kill bacteria and deaden pain.

34) If a capuchin monkey has an itch it will scratch itself hard with a fuzzy seedpod until the scratchy hairs are worn off the pod. It will then discard the useless seedpod and get another.

35) White-nosed coatis rub resin from the trattinnickia tree into their coats. The menthol-like smelling resin repels fleas, lice, ticks and mosquitoes.

36) Black, brown and kodiak bears make up a herbal paste out of osha roots. They use this as a topical anaesthetic and antibacterial.

37) Cats don't just roll in catnip for fun. They do it because it helps repel pests. The plant's ingredients are insecticidal.

38) The European hedgehog is vulnerable to fleas and ticks and cannot groom itself for obvious reasons. So it anoints itself with mint, oil, and fermenting fruit. It uses its own saliva too, using its tongue to flick enriched saliva over its body.

39) Birds roll in dust to soak up excess feather oil. This helps by making their skin dry and less hospitable to mites. When birds lift their wings they are doing so to expose the underside to sunlight and, thereby, kill bacteria.

40) Capuchin monkeys sometimes wash themselves with their own urine. They do this because urea (a main component of urine) is an antibacterial and antifungal and has a stronger cooling effect than water alone

41) Tannin rich plants are astringent, they make the mouth feel dry and they don't taste very nice. Most grazing animals avoid them. But tannin rich plants are antiseptic, antibacterial, antifungal, antidiarrhoeal and antihelmintic. And so animals which are ill will often choose to eat these plants in order to treat themselves.

Chapter 3   Animals Protect Themselves From Insects

Insect bites aren't just irritating; biting insects spread malaria, bubonic plague, sleeping sickness, dengue, filariasis, yellow fever and many more diseases. Just six blood sucking ticks can kill a gazelle. Malaria, estimated to have killed half the people who have ever lived, is spread by mosquitoes. A horse can lose up to half a litre of blood a day to blood sucking flies.

Recognising this danger, animals do many things to protect themselves.

1) North American caribou avoid mosquitoes by huddling together on small patches of ice.

2) Wild horses move to windy hills where the grazing is poor but flies find it difficult to land

3) Elephants, rhinoceroses and buffalo are all susceptible to blood suckers (despite their thick hides) so they roll in mud for protection. Malay elephants carry palm leaves in their trunks to flick away flies. Elephants in Nepal have been seen to strip off excess leaves in order to make a fly swatter with the right length and flexibility.

4) Tigers lie in water with just their heads above the surface.

5) Chimpanzees use leafy twigs to swat flies.

6) A horse being bothered by flies will gallop around, roll in the mud, shake its head and flick its tail to get rid of flies.

7) Animals hang around forest fires because there are no flies.

8) Camels in the desert (where there are no trees or fence posts for rubbing against) will rub against one another.

9) Elephants can twitch their skin so powerfully that insects are trapped and killed in their skin folds.

10) Herons peck at mosquitoes at the rate of 3,000 an hour.

11) Primates groom one another, picking out parasites and sometimes eating the insects they've found.

12) The female wood mouse will sometimes only allow a male to have sex with her after he has groomed her and got rid of her ticks.

13) Mated penguins groom one another and have fewer ticks than solitary birds.

14) When impalas groom one another for ticks they take turns. 'You remove my ticks, I'll remove yours.'

15) Some animals help creatures of another species. So, for example, black caracara birds clean the ticks from bare-skinned tapirs.

Chapter 4   Animals Are Capable Of Love

Animals are just as capable as human beings of loving their partners, their families, their children, their leaders, their teachers, their friends and others who are important to them. An ape will show exactly the same signs of love and affection when dealing with her baby as a human mother will when dealing with her baby. Both will look longingly, tickle and play with their baby. Both feed their young, wash them, risk their lives for them and willingly put up with their noise and unruly behaviour.

Anyone who doubts that animals love their young should stand outside a farmyard when a calf has been taken away from a cow and listen to the heartbreaking cries of anguish which result. Cows have been known to trek miles to try to reach a calf from whom they have been parted.

Even fish will risk their lives to protect their young. In his seminal work *The Universal Kinship* (first published in 1906) J. Howard Moore described how he put his hand into a pond near the nest of a perch. The courageous fish guarding the nest chased Moore's hand away several times and nipped it vigorously when it was not removed quickly enough.

Lewis Gompertz, who lived from 1779 to 1861 and was a potent champion of the rights of blacks, women and the poor (and, indeed, all oppressed human beings) was also a powerful champion of animals. He was a founder of the Royal Society for the Prevention of Cruelty to Animals. In his book *Moral Inquiries On the Situation*

Of Man And Of Brutes Gompertz wrote: 'From some birds we may learn real constancy in conjugal affection, though in most instances their contracts only last for one season, but how strict do they keep this. They have no laws, no parchments, no parsons, no fear to injuring their characters, not even their own words to break in being untrue to each other: but their virtue is their laws, their parchments, their parsons, and their reputation; their deeds are their acts, their acts - their deeds: and from their own breasts do they honestly tear down to line the beds of their legitimate offspring.'

Gompertz described an incident illustrating the wisdom of blackbirds. 'I observed a male blackbird flying about in an extreme state of agitation,' he wrote. 'And on my going to discover the cause of it, the bird retreated from me as I followed it, till it stopped at a nest containing a female bird sitting upon her eggs, near which there was a cat: in consequence of this I removed the cat, and the bird became quiet. After that, whenever the cat was about the place, the blackbird would come near my window, and would in the same manner direct me to some spot where the cat happened to be stationed.' Gompertz also described other three incidents which illustrate animal kindness and wisdom. The first concerned two goats which had met each other on a narrow path between two precipices. There was no room for the two goats to turn or pass and so one of the goats lay down, allowing the other to walk over it. The second incident involved a horse who had been hurt by a nail when he had been shod. Finding it painful to walk he returned to the farrier and showed him his hoof. The third incident involved a sheep dog who jumped into freezing cold water and successfully rescued another dog which had been floating on a lump of ice. 'I would now fain ask,' wrote Gompertz, 'if all this does not show reason and virtue?'

A woman who keeps rats has reported how when one rat was too ill to fetch food for herself a second rat brought food from their bowl into the nest where the sick rat was lying and laid the food around her so that she could eat without having to move. Every time the woman tried to pick up the sick rat, the nurse rat, doubtless misunderstanding her motives, bit her hand.

J. Howard Moore described how monkeys may adopt the orphans of deceased members of their tribe and how two crows fed a third crow which was wounded. The wound was several weeks old and the two crows had clearly been playing `good Samaritans' for that time.

Charles Darwin wrote about a blind pelican which was fed with fish which were brought to it by pelican friends who normally lived thirty miles away.

And strong males in a herd of vicunas will lag behind to protect the weaker and slower members of their herd from possible predators.

Before slavery was abolished, black people who fell in love were regarded as enjoying simple `animal lust' as a result of `animal attraction'. When black people formed life long pairs this was dismissed as nothing more than a response to an `instinct'. The same things are, of course, said about animals (with just as little evidence to support it). Animal abusers argue that animals which seem to show love are merely acting according to instinct. However, the evidence proves that animals are perfectly capable of feeling complex emotions. Animals are certainly capable of loving. Many animals are so loyal to one another that if one half of a couple dies the other may die shortly afterwards - consumed by grief. This has been reported to happen with swans, wolves and oxen. Here are some examples:

1) A statue of a small Akita dog named Hachiko stands prominently in the forecourt of Japan's busiest railway station. Every morning, Hachiko would accompany his master to his train to work and arrive again at the end of the day to greet his master from his return journey. Sadly, Hachiko's master did not make the return journey one evening because he had suffered a fatal heart attack while at work. But Hachiko still waited patiently for his master to return. Hachiko returned at the same time the following day in the hope that his master would step off the train to greet him. Hachiko soon became well-known to local commuters who would often stop to lavish affection on the small dog and give him treats. For an

incredible nine years, Hachiko waited every evening in the hope that his master would return. When Hachiko died, the Japanese erected a statue of him in his honour to commemorate his love and devotion.

2) A Friesian cow called Daisy was sold for auction in Okehampton in Devon, England. Daisy was so upset about being parted from her new calf that she jumped over her enclosure and ran the six miles back home to be with her calf.

3) A cow called Emma was so distraught that her calf had been taken away from her that she made it her mission to find her baby. Just before milking time, Emma escaped from the field where she was kept and ran the four miles to the abattoir where her calf was about to be slaughtered. She made such a fuss when she got there that staff admitted to being afraid. Suddenly, one of the calves in line to be slaughtered recognised its mother's cries and ran frantically towards her. Emma was so happy to be reunited with her calf that she couldn't stop licking and nuzzling her baby. Touched by what had happened, the abattoir workers contacted Emma's owner who took pity on the mother and calf and decided to keep them both.

4) In 1988, Molly Parfett's husband died in hospital after suffering from a massive stroke. Shortly after the funeral, Molly noticed that their dog, Joe, would disappear for hours at a time. She discovered that Joe was to be found sitting by his master's grave. Molly had no idea how Joe knew where her husband was buried.

5) There is a monument near Derwent Dam in Derbyshire, England, with the following inscription: `In Commemoration of the devotion of Tip the sheepdog who stayed by the body of her dead master, Mr Joseph Tagg, on the Howden Moor for fifteen weeks from 12th December 1953 to 27th March 1954.'

6) Farmer Alfred Gruenemeyer, who lived near Coburg in central Germany, treated his animals more like pets than livestock. And so when Gruenemeyer died, his animals were devastated. A young bull called Barnaby was so distressed that he left his field, walked for a mile, leapt the cemetery wall, found the farmer's grave and started a vigil which lasted for several days. Attempts to chase the young bull

away failed when locals discovered just how unnerving an angry bull can be. It wasn't until several days later that the bull calmed down and could be led back to his pasture. Mr Gruenemeyer was said by neighbours to have allowed his animals to roam in and out of his house. 'He talked to them like Dr Dolittle,' said one. 'Mind you, his house smelled a bit.'

Chapter 5   Animals Are Sentient Creatures

A surprising number of apparently intelligent individuals (including, of course, a variety of vivisectors, hunters and butchers) excuse the cruel way they treat animals by claiming that animals don't have feelings. (Hunt supporters claim that foxes are not sentient but that they 'enjoy' being hunted!)

The truth, as anyone who is capable of reading and observing will know, is that animals *are* sentient and exhibit many of those qualities which some people like to think of as being the preserve of the human race. Charles Darwin showed that fear produces similar responses in both humans and animals. The eyes and mouth open, the heart beats rapidly, teeth chatter, muscles tremble, hairs stand on end and so on. Parrots, like human beings, turn away and cover their eyes when confronted with a sight which overwhelms them. Young elephants who have seen their families killed by poachers wake up screaming in the night. Elephants who are suddenly separated from their social group may die suddenly of 'broken heart syndrome'. Apes may fall down and faint when suddenly coming across a snake.

If a man shouts at a dog the dog will often cower and back away in fear.

The fact is that many animals are brighter than many people. We do not abuse babies simply because they cannot speak or finish *The Times* crossword while having breakfast. Why, then, do our rules of behaviour allow us to assume that we have the authority to abuse animals? Animals have passionate relationships with one another, they exhibit clear signs of love, they develop social lives which are every bit as complex as our own. Animals frequently make friends across the species barriers and there is much evidence showing that animals have helped animals belonging to different species. Animals are often compassionate and are clearly sentient.

Chapter 6   Animals As Teachers

There is now no doubt that animals actively teach their young in order to pass on skills which many traditionally regarded as being 'nothing more than instinct'.

So, for example, we have watched an adult cat giving lessons to orphan kittens for which he had taken responsibility. The adult cat, teaching the art of stalking, would edge forwards and then stop and look over his shoulder to see if the kittens were following in the correct style. After the lesson had gone on for some time the kittens started playing behind the adult cat's back. They got away with it a couple of times but on the third occasion the adult cat saw them. He reached back and gave them both a clip with an outstretched paw. The kittens weren't hurt but they paid attention to what they were being taught.

Chapter 7 Animals As Carers: How Animals Help People

It is well known that animals help people in a number of different ways. People who would otherwise be lonely but who share their lives with a dog or a cat often suffer far less from illness than those who do not have an animal to talk to or sit with. Stroking a cat can help reduce blood pressure. Talking to a budgerigar can help stave off depression. Watching goldfish swimming around a tank can ease anxiety. And walking the dog can help ease aching joints and improve cardiovascular fitness.

But here are some other examples of how compassionate, thoughtful, imaginative and caring animals can and do help people.

1) In *When Elephants Weep* Jeffrey Masson and Susan McCarthy report how a man called John Teal, who was working with endangered musk oxen, was alarmed when some dogs approached. Immediately, the oxen formed a defensive ring around him and lowered their horns at the dogs. It turned out that the musk oxen

were protecting their new human friend in exactly the same way that they would protect their calves from predators.

2) The life of a man in Boston, USA, was saved by his dog Belle who had been trained to call for help. The man, who was diabetic had a seizure and collapsed. The dog then bit into the unconscious man's cell phone and called the emergency services on 911.

3) Dogs can help diabetic patients by using their keen sense of smell. The dogs can detect abnormalities in a diabetic's blood sugar levels. For example, one specially trained dog periodically licked her owner's nose to check his blood sugar level. If she was worried (because she could smell ketones) she would paw and whine at him until he took action to put things right. `Every time she paws at me in that way I grab my meter and test myself,' said the man. `She's never been wrong.'

4) A dog's nose has 220 million cells associated with its sense of smell. Humans have just 5 million. (It is for this reason that dogs are used to sniff out drugs, explosives and human remains.) Some experts now even claim that dogs can be trained to smell cancer cells in human beings. Dr Armand Gognetta, a skin cancer specialist, has reported that a grey-haired Schnauzer called George, who has been trained to detect skin cancer cells in humans, has a success rate of nearly 100%. George was trained after a medical journal had described how another dog had kept sniffing at a particular mole on her owner's leg - ignoring a number of other moles. A biopsy revealed that the mole which had attracted attention had been malignant.

5) Dogs have been reported to be sensitive to impending epileptic seizures. No one knows how they do this but dogs are sensitive to seizures about 40 minutes before they occur. Dogs can therefore be trained to offer early warnings - enabling their owners to take the appropriate precautions for their safety.

6) Many pets know (presumably through some sixth sense such as extra sensory perception) that their owners are going to be in danger. Wildlife writer George Laycock has described how a collie whose

owner worked in an explosives factory, tried to save his owner's life. Every day the collie walked to work with the man. But, one day, the dog began to whine and sat down in the road. The dog would not budge. Eventually the man left the dog and went to work alone. The collie went back home and crawled under the man's bed. He stayed there all day, whining. That day a tremendous explosion destroyed the factory - and killed the collie's owner.

7) Cat owners have reported that when they are feeling ill their cat will make much of a fuss of them - purring loudly and rubbing against them when they are feeling unwell.

8) It has frequently been reported that dogs who are separated from their owners will sense when something terrible has happened. Author Sandra Collier reports that when a friend was taken seriously ill while on holiday her dogs, left at home in the care of another friend, began howling in the middle of the night. The dogs howled continuously. It was later discovered that the dogs had started howling at the moment their owner had fallen ill.

9) Writer Ernest Thompson Seton got caught in two wolf traps while working in the wilderness. At nightfall, a pack of hungry wolves gathered around him. The leader began to growl and snap at Seton who was trapped and helpless. As the wolves were about to attack, Seton's dog Bingo suddenly appeared and killed the leader of the wolf pack. Bingo then dragged a tool to Seton that enabled him to undo the traps and free himself. The really strange thing is that the dog had not been taken on Seton's expedition. At home he had whimpered and acted strangely. Eventually, despite attempts to detain him, he had headed into the dark to find the endangered Seton.

10) Four New Zealanders were swimming off Ocean Beach near Whangarei on New Zealand's North Island when dolphins swam close to them in tight circles and herded them to safety. One of the swimmers, a lifesaver, tried to escape from the dolphins but was herded back into the group - just as he noticed a nine foot great white shark swimming towards them. 'The dolphins had corralled us up to protect us,' said the lifesaver. The swimmers spent the next 40

minutes surrounded by the dolphins. When the shark disappeared they were allowed to swim back to shore. The dolphins had sensed the danger to the human swimmers and had taken action to protect them, just as they would protect their young. Later, two of the dolphins were butchered by poachers.

11) Animals have been known to give food to hungry humans. Koko, the gorilla who learned to communicate with humans through sign language, gave medical advice to a woman who complained of indigestion. Koko told the woman to drink orange juice. When the human revisited ten days later and offered Koko a drink of orange juice Koko would not accept the drink until assured that the woman felt better.

12) A Border collie woke a young mother from a deep sleep and led her to her baby's cot. The baby was choking on mucus and had stopped breathing.

13) Two women and ten children lived in very poor conditions in Naples, Italy. They had to share one room. Despite their extreme poverty, and unbelievably cramped living space, they still managed to make room for a stray dog whom they named Rocky. One spring afternoon, two of the children, aged three and six, were left on their own with Rocky. A fire broke out. Rocky fought through the flames, grabbed one of the girls by her dress and dragged her out into the street. Realising that the other little girl was still in the building, Rocky braved the flames again and the second little girl emerged safely. But this time Rocky did not come with the girl. Sadly, the dog was found dead inside the room with his fur alight. He had died from smoke inhalation.

14) In 1989, teenager Adam Maguire was surfing off the north coast of Sydney, Australia, when a 12-foot shark suddenly attacked him. The shark sank his teeth into the teenager's side. Once sharks have tasted blood they invariably want more. Adam Maguire's friends could only watch in horror. But just as the shark was about to move in for the kill, a school of dolphins isolated the shark then chased it away. Thanks to them Adam Maguire survived.

15) A golden Labrador called Sally loved her 79-year-old blind master so much that she willingly sacrificed her life for him. Bill Chamberlain was about to be hit by an oncoming car when his guide dog Sally stepped in and pushed him out of the way so that he wouldn't get run over. It was Sally who died.

16) In the 1980s, 81-year-old Norman Stephenson from Bradford, England, left his home to go for a walk along the steep Pennine hillside. At the same time a dog called Laska also made her way to the same hillside after escaping from her owners' house. When it began to rain heavily, Mr Stephenson slipped and fell down into a ditch. Laska found him and used her body to protect the stranger from the foul weather. Hikers stumbled across the pair the next day and raised the alarm. Thanks to Laska, Mr Stephenson lived to tell the incredible tale. And Laska was reunited with her worried owners.

17) Nipper, a five-year-old collie, bravely rescued his animal friends when fire broke out at his owners' farm in Sussex, England. Nipper boldly made his way back and forth through the smoke to shepherd lambs and calves to safety. The brave collie received blisters to his paws and singed his fur.

18) When brother and sister, Sean and Erin Callahan, were out playing near their home in Texas, USA they came across a rattlesnake. The rattlesnake was about to attack when Leo their four-year-old poodle quickly stood between the children and the snake. As a result of Leo's heroism, the children managed to escape. Amazingly, the poodle survived despite being bitten six times on the head.

19) A dog called Bruce saved a four-year-old Welsh boy from sinking into mud and drowning. When the boy sank above his waist in riverside mud, Bruce lay on his side and clasped the boy's shoulder between his teeth to prevent him from sinking any further. Thankfully, the boy's mother spotted their dilemma and called for help.

20) While out bathing in Lake Sommersville in Texas, USA, Priscilla the pig spotted a young boy in trouble. Priscilla quickly

swam towards the boy and used her snout to keep his head above the water. When the boy clutched her collar, Priscilla brought the boy safely to shore.

21) Ray and his fiancée were out on a nature trail walk with their dog, Woodie, when Ray decided to climb a nearby cliff to take some photographs. When Ray was out of view, Woodie pulled frantically on his lead. When he had managed to break free, he ran up the cliff and also disappeared from sight. Ray's fiancée followed their trail and to her horror she saw her fiancé lying unconscious in a stream at the bottom of the cliff, with Woodie by his side. Woodie had jumped off the cliff to save his owner and was nudging Ray's head to keep it above the water and prevent him from drowning. Despite their injuries, Ray and Woodie survived.

22) Carletta the cow saved her owner, Bruno Cipriano, from being gored to death by a boar at his farm in Tuscany, Italy. Carletta charged at the boar and used her horns to head-butt it until the boar ran away.

Chapter 8   Animals Can Use Tools

Humans like to think (rather arrogantly) that only they can think and use tools. Some may find that this sense of superiority makes it easier to use and abuse animals for their own benefit. Many allegedly eminent scientists still deny that animals can make tools. There is no doubt that this viewpoint makes them very popular with the meat industry and with scientific laboratories where animals are used in experiments. But the truth is rather different. The truth is that many animals use sticks and stones as implements to help them in their daily lives.

1) Insects use small stones to pack the dirt firmly over and around their nests.

2) Spiders use stones to keep their webs steady when the weather is stormy.

3) Orangutans and baboons use sticks and stones as weapons.

4) Monkeys use stones to help them crack nuts. In one zoo a monkey who had poor teeth kept (and guarded) a stone hidden in its straw for nut cracking. That monkey had a tool which it regarded as its own property.

5) Chimpanzees drum on hollow logs with sticks in order to send messages to one another.

6) Monkeys know how to use sticks as levers.

7) The Indian elephant will break off a leafy branch and use it to sweep away flies.

8) A lurcher called Red at Battersea Dogs Home in London, England, startled staff by using his teeth to open the spring-loaded catch on his kennel. He would wait until the staff had gone home and locked up for the night before escaping. Once free he would then pad along the corridor and free his chums before leading them to the food store for midnight feasts. This happened a dozen times before the humans found out how the animals were escaping.

9) At Oxford University a crow called Betty picked up a piece of wire, used her beak to shape it and bent it into a hook to lift food from the bottom of a vertical pipe. Once she had learned how to do this she made other hooks to extract food from places she couldn't

reach with her beak or claws. She did this without being shown how to do it.

10) Chimpanzees routinely use tools such as twigs and stones to help them hunt and gather food. Scientists from England's Cambridge University watched animals for several months in southern Senegal. Chimpanzees were observed making spears out of tree branches and then using their spears to catch small wild animals such as bush babies (creatures the size of squirrels). The chimpanzees first selected a branch of the right length, then removed the leaves and trimmed off extra branches. They then used their teeth to whittle the end of the spear to a sharp point. The chimpanzees used one hand to direct the spear - much as a human will.

11) Gorillas use branches to test the depth of water they intend to wade through.

12) Gorillas use giant leaves as napkins to clean their fingers and faces after eating - particularly when they've been eating messy fruits.

13) Crows are cunning birds who have great skills with tools. They have been seen using leaves as probes to extract grubs from crevices. A study published by experts at the University of Auckland has shown that, like humans and some other larger animals, crows can use a combination of tools. The birds use logic and reasoning to decide how best to get what they want. So for example, they will use one tool (a short stick) to create or obtain a second tool (a longer stick) which they need to reach food.

14) Monkeys use tools to dig up roots, crack seeds and dig insects out of holes in trees. Two scientists from Cambridge watched wild Capuchin monkeys in the Sierra da Capivara National Park in northeastern Brazil and discovered that their use of tools is widespread. Stones were used as spades to dig up roots or other food, to crack open seeds, break tubers into smaller more manageable pieces for eating and to open hollow branches. The monkeys also used stones to crush lizards and to break the outer hard skin of cactus plants in order to get at the soft, edible inside of the

plant. The monkeys were seen to use a stone in one hand, for digging, while using the other hand for moving away loosened soil. Most remarkable of all, perhaps, was the fact that the monkeys were seen to improve their tools. When using twigs to probe tree holes or crevices in rocks in order to reach honey, insects or water they would modify the twigs by breaking off leaves or stems to make them more useful.

Chapter 9   Animals Eat The Foods They Need

Animals living in the wild are very good at adapting to their wild surroundings and ensuring that they have a balanced diet. They adapt their diet according to what is available and in order to obtain the essential nutrients their bodies need.

1) Fallow deer eat grass in the summer and browse on fruits such as acorns in the autumn. During the winter they eat ivy, holly and brambles. Then, in the spring, when the grass starts to grow they start eating grass again.

2) Wildebeests migrate from lush grass of the north of the Serengeti Plains of Tanzania when they have calves. They go to the southern plains and to the foothills of volcanoes where they eat grass growing on ash rich soils. The grass there is rich in calcium and phosphorus (both of which are necessary for lactation).

3) In California, desert tortoises travel long distances to find calcium, which they consume in vast quantities. They need the calcium to keep their shells strong.

4) Rats need extra calcium during pregnancy and lactation. So they deliberately eat more calcium rich foods at those times. Their bodies help by absorbing more calcium from the food available.

5) Moose need large quantities of calcium and phosphorus for their antlers. Without the necessary minerals they are likely to suffer from osteoporosis as their growing antlers take the calcium and phosphorus from their bones. To avoid this problem they chew on old, cast off antlers to get the minerals they need. Similarly, reindeer, who also need calcium and phosphorus for antler growing (as well as for milk production), will chew on old antlers. They will also eat soil from around decayed bones.

6) Camels and giraffe (both of which are, like moose and reindeer, vegetarian) have been known to eat the bones of dead animals in order to obtain essential minerals.

7) Sheep in the Shetland Islands have been known to eat ground nesting birds - and so have red deer in the Hebrides. In both cases the normally vegetarian animals ate the birds in order to obtain essential minerals which were temporarily missing from their normal diet. Red deer have also been seen to eat small rabbits. Caribou have been known to eat lemmings and white-tailed deer have been seen eating fish.

8) In the jungles of Malaysia, elephants have been seen drinking water from the bottom of a spring pool because there was more sulphur there.

9) In Scotland, reindeer have been known to lick and chew at salt preserved canvas tents.

10) In Africa, buffalo have been seen licking other buffalo which were sweating in order to replenish their salt supplies.

11) Dogs, and other animals which live with humans, will lick toilet bowls to obtain the salt in urine.

12) Moose will eat aquatic plants such as water lilies because they are rich in sodium.

13) Biologist and author Lyall Watson reported seeing a herd of cattle eating and licking at the bark of a tree. When he examined the tree he found that the tree had a copper nail embedded in the bark. The cattle were all copper deficient.

14) Sheep which have access to a fully varied diet, can adjust their feeding to make sure that they have the right mixture of protein and carbohydrate. They can also adjust their diet to ensure that they repair any mineral deficiencies.

15) Animals don't just eat foods their bodies need. They will sometimes flavour their foods to increase their enjoyment. An Indian elephant living in a zoo used to split an apple into two and then rub the two halves onto hay to flavour it.

16) Herbivores are very good at avoiding toxic plants. Bracken fern comes in two forms - one of which contains toxic cyanide. Both red deer and sheep avoid the bracken that contains the cyanide but eat the bracken that doesn't. Voles can discriminate between clovers that contain cyanide and clovers that don't. If they have no alternative but to eat the clover containing the cyanide they just eat less of it.

17) Anyone who doubts that animals have a powerful sense of taste should try putting a pill into a cat's meal. Cats are very good at detecting toxins and will eat round them.

18) Rats increase their consumption of a food if they see other rats eating it, or if they smell that another rat has been nearby. If they find a new food that no other rats have eaten they will taste it, wait to see if they develop problems and only go back and eat the rest if they don't become ill.

19) A baby elephant will find out which foods are safe to eat by taking food from its mother's mouth and tasting it.

20) Some foods are harmful to mice but, if eaten in the right proportions, they are safe because the toxins in one cancel out the toxins in the other. Mice manage to adjust their diet to ensure that they get the balance right.

Chapter 10   Animals Have Feelings

Monkeys have a well-developed sense of grievance. Sarah Brosnan and Frans de Waal of Emory University in Atlanta, Georgia in the USA, studied the behaviour of female brown capuchin monkeys and spent two years teaching them to exchange tokens for food. So, for example, monkeys were allowed to exchange small pieces of rock for slices of cucumber. This worked well some of the time. However, when one monkey was handed a grape in return for a token her neighbour was reluctant to hand over her token for a mere piece of cucumber. (In the world of the capuchin monkey a grape is infinitely more attractive than a piece of cucumber. It is the Choo sandal compared to the utility slipper.)

Monkeys who got short changed became sulky and sullen and even tossed their tokens away in disgust. In some circumstances monkeys even forfeited food that they could see - and would normally have happily accepted - solely because they felt aggrieved. Monkeys, like humans, operate in social circles. When one monkey feels cheated, the system breaks down. Righteous indignation is not something exclusively found among humans.

It isn't just monkeys who have such feelings. Observers at England's Bristol University discovered that cows bear grudges, form friendships, enjoy intellectual challenges, experience happiness, worry about the future and feel pain and fear.

Chapter 11   Animals Have Powerful Homing Instincts

Like birds, many animals have remarkable homing skills. Using the earth's magnetic field, the angle of the sun and its own biological clock an animal which is taken from its home can find its way back over remarkably long distances. Cats in particular seem to have an astonishing ability to find their way home. (There is some evidence that human beings used to have this skill, have lost it, but can regain it if they try.) There are many well-authenticated stories of animals who have found their way home across vast distances. Here are just a few:

1) After she was sent to Nebraska in the USA, a cat called Cookie travelled 550 miles to get back to her home in Chicago.

2) A cat called Howie travelled across 1,000 miles of wilderness and desert in the Australian outback to find his owner when she moved home. Howie's adventure included crossing several rivers.

3) When truck driver, Geoff Hancock, stopped at a café 1800 miles away from his home, his fox terrier called Whisky jumped out of the vehicle. It was nine months before Whisky finally arrived safely home after travelling solo for 1800 miles.

4) A cat called Tom crossed the USA, travelling 2,500 miles from Florida to California, in order to find his owners in their new home. His journey took him just over two years.

5) Kuzya, a Russian cat, travelled 1,300 miles across Siberia to get back together with the people he lived with. Kuzya got lost when his family were travelling on holiday. After weeks of desperate searching, the humans eventually gave up and went home. But Kuzya turned up three months later in perfect health.

6) Ken Phillips and his teenage son lost their cat, Silky, at Gin Gin in Australia. Over six months later, Silky arrived at the family home in Melbourne, Australia after covering a distance of approximately 1,500 miles.

7) While Barbara Paule was driving her truck in Ohio, USA, her cat, Muddy Water White, jumped out of the truck and disappeared. Three years later, Muddy Water White turned up on Barbara's doorstep - 400 miles away from the spot where she vanished from the truck. Muddy was so dishevelled that it took his owner three days to recognise him.

8) After Murka the tortoiseshell cat had killed several pet canaries, her owner sent her 400 miles to live with his mother. A couple of days later, Murka disappeared from her new abode. Murka returned to her original home pregnant and reportedly hungry (presumably for canaries).

9) A snake which was carried a hundred miles away from home managed to find its way back.

10) An English Setter called Bede got lost while holidaying in Cornwall, England, with his owner, Louis Heston. Six months later, Bede turned up at his owner's home after travelling a distance of more than 300 miles.

11) During World War I a man called Jones-Brown enlisted in the army and, naturally, had to leave his dog Prince, an Irish terrier, behind with his family in Ireland. Prince became depressed and would not eat. When he was taken on a trip to England with the family, the dog disappeared. Mrs Jones-Brown wrote to her husband to tell him the sad news that his dog had gone. Her husband wrote back to tell her that Prince was with him. The dog had somehow managed to cross the English Channel and find his master.

Chapter 12   Animals Have Powerful Imaginations

There is plenty of evidence to show that many creatures other than human beings have powerful imaginations.

1) Cats, dogs and horses and many other creatures dream.

2) Parrots talk in their sleep.

3) Horses frequently stampede because they are frightened by objects (such as large rocks or posts) which are no real threat to them. This must show a sense of imagination because the horse, like a child, has created a terror out of nothing.

4) A cat playing with a ball of wool imagines that it is hunting.

5) Spiders will hold down the edges of their webs with stones to steady them during gales which have not yet started. Does this show an ability to predict the weather or imagination?

Chapter 13   Animals Enjoy Playing

We accept that cats and dogs like to play (though, quite erroneously, often assuming that it is because we have taught them how to do it) but we usually reject the notion that other animals play. So, for example, when we see dolphins leaping in the sea scientists tell us that they are communicating; sending messages to other dolphins. When we point out that sheep and lambs like to play the same sort of games that children play, cynics accuse us of being anthropomorphic. (A few minutes observation will confirm that lambs play tag, king of the castle, hide and seek and even enjoy running races. Even fully-grown sheep enjoy playing together - abandoning their more active games only when arthritis prevents them from moving easily.) The problem is that most people never stop to watch animals for long enough. And the people who do have the opportunity to watch, farmers and hunters, don't like to admit that the creatures they kill so readily are sentient and playful. And so they sustain their ignorance by refusing to see what they look at. The truth is that human beings are not the only animals to have a sense of humour and fun and to enjoy playing games. Foxes will tease hyenas by going close to them and then running away. Ravens tease peregrine falcons by flying closer and closer to them. Grebes tweak the tails of dignified swans and then dive to escape. A monkey has been seen to pass his hand behind a second monkey so that he could tweak the tail of a third monkey. When the third monkey remonstrated with the second monkey the first monkey - the practical joker - was clearly enjoying himself. Ants, fish, birds, horses, lions, porpoises and many other creatures have all been observed playing games. And some animals can be very imaginative when they want to play. Farmers living in Wales couldn't understand how their sheep were escaping over cattle grids without getting their feet or legs trapped. The sheep were constantly escaping and playing with wild ponies on nearby moorland. Eventually the farmers lay in wait to see how the sheep were escaping. To their amazement the sheep were simply lying down and rolling over the cattle grids. No one but the sheep had thought of that.

Chapter 14   Why Animals Hide Their Pain To Protect Themselves

Scientists often deny that animals suffer pain and claim that the evidence for this assertion is the fact that animals don't react in the way that people do when they are in pain. People in pain often cry out or show other signs of distress but animals usually remain quiet and will suffer great pain apparently stoically.

The reason for this is simple. As far as animals are concerned there is often no advantage to them in showing to humans that they are feeling pain. On the contrary, there are good reasons to disguise that they are in pain. Wounded animals try to hide their pain from predators and to many animals, human beings are predators. Animals know that if they show that they are in pain (and therefore weak) they will be more vulnerable to attack. In addition, animals who live in hierarchical societies (such as lions) may lose status if they appear to be in distress.

However, if they are loved and well cared for, animals will show their pain and distress to those whom they trust.

Curiously, the same scientists who deny that animals ever feel pain, frequently perform laboratory experiments designed to test new pain killing drugs on animals. If animals feel no pain, what is the point of the experiments?

Chapter 15 Animals Have Their Own Pets

Animals have often been reported to have pets of their own.

A chimpanzee who was thought to be lonely was given a kitten as a companion. The chimpanzee groomed the kitten, carried it about with her and protected it from harm.

A gorilla called Koko had a kitten companion which she herself named All Ball.

An elephant was seen to routinely put aside some grain for a mouse to eat.

Racehorses who have had goat companions have failed to run as expected when separated from their friends.

Chapter 16   Animals Can Be Self-Conscious

Animals have often been reported to show signs of self-consciousness, embarrassment and other allegedly exclusively human emotions.

1) Chimpanzees have been observed using a TV video monitor to watch themselves making faces. The chimpanzees were able to distinguish between a live image and a taped image by testing to see if their actions were duplicated on the screen. Chimpanzees have even managed to use a video monitor to help them apply make up to themselves (humans find that this is a difficult trick to learn). One chimpanzee has been reported to have used a video camera and monitor to look down his own throat - using a flashlight to help the process.

2) A gorilla who had a number of toy dolls used sign language to send kisses to her favourite. But every time she realised that she was being watched she stopped doing this - presumably through embarrassment.

3) When a bottlenose porpoise accidentally bit her trainer's hand she became `hideously embarrassed', went to the bottom of her tank with her snout in a corner, and wouldn't come out until the trainer made it clear that she wasn't cross.

4) Wild chimpanzees show embarrassment and shame and may show off to other animals whom they want to impress.

5) People who live with cats will have probably noticed that if a cat falls off a piece of furniture it will immediately do something else, as though pretending that the fall didn't take place at all - often beginning to wash itself.

6) Elephant keepers report that when elephants are laughed at they will respond by filling their trunks with water and spraying the people who are laughing at them.

7) Many dog owners have reported that their animals make it clear that they know when they have done wrong. A dog which feels it has behaved badly may go into a submissive position before its pack leader (or `owner') knows that the animal has done something `bad'.

Chapter 17   Animals Can Be Artistic

We don't usually think of animals as having artistic natures. But this is simply because of our prejudices. When a bird takes bright objects to decorate its nest we tend to dismiss this as pointless theft though when a human being collects bird feathers to decorate a room or a hat they are said to be showing artistic tendencies. Here are half a dozen well-documented examples of animals exhibiting artistic tendencies.

1) Naturalist Gerald Durrell wrote about a pigeon who listened quietly to most types of music but who would stamp backwards and forwards when marches were being played and would twist and bow, cooing softly, when waltzes were played.

2) A gorilla enjoyed the singing of tenor Luciano Pavarotti so much that he would refuse to go out of doors when a Pavarotti concert was being shown on television.

3) Animal abusers have for years dismissed bird song as merely mating calls. But it is now suspected that birds sing to give themselves pleasure.

4) Numerous apes have painted or drawn identifiable objects while in captivity.

5) When a young Indian elephant was reported to have made numerous drawings (which were highly commended by artists who did not know that the artist was an animal) other zookeepers reported that their elephants often scribbled on the ground with sticks or stones. When an Asian elephant got extra attention because of her paintings, nearby African elephants used the ends of logs to draw on the walls of their enclosure.

Chapter 18   Animals Have Good Memories

Many animals have excellent memories. Chimpanzees, for example, have much better memories than human beings and outperformed university students in memory tests devised by Japanese scientists. The tasks involved remembering the location of numbers on a screen and correctly recalling the sequence. Researchers at Kyoto University tested 12 students and three chimps who had been taught the numbers one to nine. The numbers were shown on a computer screen and were obscured with white squares after each participant touched the first number. The aim was to touch all the squares in ascending order. The chimps finished this task faster than the humans with exactly the same accuracy. When the test was repeated at a faster speed, the best chimp scored 80% while the best human managed only 40% accuracy. When the best chimp was matched against a human memory champion, the chimp managed a 90% score compared to the human champion's 33%. (The human memory champion could memorise the order of a shuffled deck of cards in 30 seconds.) The findings were published in the journal *Current Biology* in December 2007. Scientists concluded that humans may have underestimated the intelligence of our closest living relatives. Other tests have shown that chimpanzees perform much better than humans on tests measuring both spatial memory and facial recognition

Even sheep, those much-derided animals, have amazing memories as described in our book *Animal Miscellany*.

'One March I got my ride-on mower out from the shed where it had been stored for the winter. I started up the engine ready to drive it across the courtyard towards the garden so that I could cut the croquet lawn. As I started up the engine I watched four sheep, who were grazing in their field, prick up their ears and start to run. I watched as they ran for several hundred yards and then stood waiting at the very spot where, the previous summer, I had dumped the grass cuttings I had taken from the lawns. It slowly dawned on me that the sheep had, after a gap of five or six months, recognised the sound of the lawn mower's engine (differentiating it from the numerous other engines they would have heard in the intervening period), recognised that the sound of the engine meant that I was about to start cutting the grass, remembered that they liked munching grass cuttings, remembered where I had dumped the grass cuttings some five or six months previously when I had last cut the lawns, and had instantly run round the field to be in position ready for the first batch of cuttings of the season. Now all that seems to suggest to me that sheep are really very bright. I know a good many human beings (most of them politicians) who could not have used that one piece of information (the starting up of a lawnmower engine) and drawn such an accurate conclusion.' – *Vernon Coleman*

Chapter 19   Animals Give One Another Presents

Giving gifts is part of the mating ritual among all sorts of animals. Even insects do it. Crickets give nuptial gifts (usually edible) designed to help win a mate and prolong copulation. Cockroaches give the female of their choice a tasty uric acid paste they have stored up for the occasion. Male scorpion flies build mounds of dried saliva which the females find irresistible. While the female eats the dried saliva the male has his wicked way with her.

Often a female will select her mate according to the size or apparent quality of the gift she is offered. Male fireflies proffer a protein boost with their sperm. The quality of the protein boost is advertised by the intensity of the firefly's glow. The male dance fly will offer a prospective lover a tasty insect nicely wrapped in silk. (Crafty dance flies will offer pretty rough looking insects very nicely wrapped. The female of the species will respond better to an ordinary gift in a beautiful wrapping than to a spectacular gift which isn't very well wrapped.)

Chapter 20   Animals Have Much Better Survival Instincts Than We Do

There has, for centuries, been a belief that animals can predict natural disasters. For example, there is good evidence that many animals know when earthquakes and tsunamis are imminent.

1) Just before the tsunami crashed into southern India in 2005, animals ran from the coast to the safety of a nearby hilltop. A herd of antelope stampeded from the shoreline ten minutes before the waves hit. In Sri Lanka, where thousands of people were killed, all the wild animals (elephants, leopards, deer, etc.) managed to survive at the Yala National Park on the coast. The animals all escaped before the waves hit. Throughout the area there was only one report of a dead animal as a result of the tsunami.

2) In California, it has been reported that horses will not let people ride them when earthquakes are due.

3) In China, in 1975, snakes emerged from hibernation to escape being buried when an earthquake hit the city of Haicheng.

4) The Chinese Government has published an official booklet describing animal signs that precede, and therefore predict, earthquakes. Tell-tale signs include cattle and horses refusing to enter their corrals, rats leaving their hiding places and running around wildly and fish jumping out of the water.

5) Before major earthquakes and floods, small mammals leave their burrows and cattle migrate to high ground.

6) Desert tortoises in the Nevada desert in the USA dig shallow holes in rocky soil to catch rain when they sense that there is a storm coming.

7) Sheep will run for shelter when they sense bad weather coming. The sky may be blue - with no signs of an impending storm - when they start running.

8) Cats can predict earthquakes. When an earthquake is coming a cat will do everything it can to get out of any building, and if they have kittens they will take the kittens with them. In the hours before an earthquake hits, cats get extremely agitated. They have often been seen scratching at doors to be let out, or simply hurrying outside. The Chinese always used to rely on cats to predict earthquakes and other natural disasters.

No one yet knows how animals do this. Do they hear or feel the rumblings of an earthquake? Do they feel the changes in the earth's electromagnetic field? Or do they sense a change in atmospheric pressure? Whatever the explanation, it seems reasonable to conclude that if you see animals running from somewhere you should leave too. If your cat suddenly picks up its kittens and heads for the door maybe you should follow.

Chapter 21   Animals Exhibit Altruistic Behaviour

Animals don't just show love; they frequently exhibit behaviour that can only be described as altruistic. Animals can suffer, they can communicate and they can care. There are numerous well-authenticated stories of animals putting their own lives at risk in order to save their loved ones.

1) Elderly lionesses who have lost their teeth and can no longer hunt, and who are too old to have young are, theoretically, of no value to the rest of the pride. But, nevertheless, the younger lions will share their kills with them. An older lioness may live out her old age - 20 years or more - being looked after by younger females.

2) A three-year-old chimpanzee is able to recognise when an adult chimpanzee (even one who is a complete stranger) needs help. And he will provide the required assistance even when there is no benefit to be gained - without expecting a reward or praise of any kind. The young chimpanzee helps simply because it wants to. For example, young, agile chimpanzees will climb trees to fetch fruit for their older relatives. Old age brings respect. Older male chimpanzees are only rarely threatened by younger animals and are tolerated without aggression. Older chimpanzees are given more grooming than they give.

3) Foxes have been observed bringing food to adult, injured foxes. When one fox was injured by a mowing machine and taken to a vet by a human observer the fox's sister took food to the spot where the injured fox had lain. The good Samaritan sister fox made the whimpering sound that foxes use when summoning cubs to eat (even though she had no cubs).

4) Whales have been observed to ask for and receive help from other whales.

5) Author J. Howard Moore described how crabs struggled for some time to turn over another crustacean which had fallen onto its back. When the crabs couldn't manage by themselves they went and fetched two other crabs to help them.

6) A gander who acted as a guardian to his blind partner would take her neck gently in his mouth and lead her to the water when she wanted to swim. Afterwards he would lead her home in the same manner. When goslings were hatched the gander, realising that the mother would not be able to cope, looked after them himself.

7) Pigs will rush to defend one of their number who is being attacked.

8) When wild geese are feeding, one will act as sentinel - never taking a grain of corn while on duty. When the sentinel goose has been on watch for a while it pecks at a nearby goose and hands over the responsibility for guarding the group.

9) When swans dive there is usually one which stays above the water to watch out for danger.

10) Time and time again dogs have pined and died on being separated from their masters or mistresses.

11) Author Konrad Lorenz described the behaviour of a gander called Ado when his mate Susanne-Elisabeth was killed by a fox. Ado stood by Susanne-Elisabeth's body in mourning. He hung his head and his body was hunched. He didn't bother to defend himself when attacked by strange geese. How would the animal abusers describe such behaviour other than as sorrow born of love? There is no survival value in mourning. It can only be a manifestation of a clear emotional response - love.

12) Coyotes form pairs before they become sexually active - and then stay together. One observer watched a female coyote licking her

partner's face after they had made love. They then curled up and went to sleep.

13) Geese, swans and mandarin ducks have all been described as enjoying long-term relationships.

14) One herd of elephants was seen to be travelling unusually slowly. Observers noted that the herd travelled slowly so as not to leave behind an elephant who had not fully recovered from a broken leg. Another herd travelled slowly to accommodate a mother who was carrying her dead calf with her. When the herd stopped to eat or drink, the mother would put her dead calf down. When they started travelling she would pick up the dead calf. The rest of the herd were accommodating her in her time of grief.

15) Vampire bats will regurgitate blood into the mouth of a sick bat.

16) Gorillas have been seen to travel slowly if one of their party is injured and unable to move quickly.

17) When animals die their relatives and friends will often bury them. A badger was seen to drag another badger - which had been killed by a car - off the road, along a hedge, through a gap and into a burial spot in nearby woods. Elephants won't pass the body of another elephant without covering the corpse with twigs, branches and earth. After scientists and park officials culled elephants in Uganda, they cut the ears and feet off the dead animals and stored them in a shed ready to be made into handbags and umbrella stands. But during the night a group of elephants broke into the shed and retrieved and then buried the ears and feet. Elephants have even been seen burying dead buffalo and dead lions.

18) If adult foxes are killed (for example, by a hunt) and they leave behind an orphaned cub, relatives of the slaughtered foxes will look after the cub. They take on responsibility as though the cub were their own.

19) Penguins keep warm in groups. When the birds on the outside begin to feel the cold they go into the centre of the group to get

warm while the warm birds, who have been huddled inside, take their turn on the outside.

20) Geese fly in changing formations to protect one another.

21) Grooming (picking fleas and bugs and mud from one another's fur) is an essential part of family life for gorillas.

22) A dwarf mongoose in the Taru desert of Kenya was badly injured. Her group stayed around her, grooming her and bringing her food until she was able to walk again.

23) Elephants will pull spears and darts out of themselves and out of each other. They will pull one another to their feet if they are having difficulty in rising.

24) Elephants have been known to rescue captured elephants in hunting raids.

25) Swiss researchers studying rats at the University of Bern discovered that rats demonstrate altruism towards strangers in much the same way that people sometimes do. People are more likely to lend a hand to a perfect stranger if they have benefited from kindness in the past and rats are just the same.

26) A researcher from the University of Parma in Italy, has shown that in Rome, where there are 350,000 stray cats in 2,000 separate colonies, male alley cats let the weakest individuals in their colony - small female cats and their kittens - eat first. The researcher concluded that the male feral cats, although normally aggressive, recognise that the weaker females and the young kittens need to be given precedence in order to survive. Of course, the cats may just have surprisingly good table manners. Whatever the explanation may be, their actions can undoubtedly be described as altruistic.

27) When around 80 whales beached themselves on New Zealand's Tokerau Beach one September day in 1983, locals tried to keep the whales alive by splashing water over them to help keep their skins moist. When the tide finally came in, the whales started to float in the right direction but soon became disorientated and beached

themselves again. There seemed to be no hope until a school of dolphins came to the rescue and successfully led the whales into the safety of the sea.

Epilogue What We Can Learn From Animals

There is much we could learn from animals if only we would open up our eyes and our minds. We don't have to experiment on animals - or to mistreat them - to learn from them. Here, are twelve things we can learn from watching how animals look after themselves and behave towards one another.

1) We should touch the people we care about as often as we can.

2) When those whom we love come home after being away, we should always hurry to greet them.

3) We should stretch when we get up before we start moving about.

4) We could soothe and protect our bodies and our minds by taking regular naps.

5) Whatever our age, we should make sure that we devote some time every day to playing.

6) Whenever we are upset or feel threatened we should avoid biting when a growl will do just as well.

7) We should forget the bad things that happen. Accept whatever punishment we may deserve. And never waste time on regrets or guilt.

8) Whatever we are doing (and however much fun it was when we started) we should always stop when we have had enough. This is particularly true of eating.

9) We should be loyal.

10) We should never pretend to be something we are not.

11) When someone we love is having a bad day, we should make sure that we sit close by to give them silent comfort.

12) We should protect the ones we love.

Appendix 1 Facts About Animal Experiments:

1) Every thirty seconds vivisectors around the world kill another thousand animals. They use cats, dogs, puppies, kittens, horses, sheep, rats, mice, guinea pigs, rabbits, monkeys, baboons and any other creature you can think of.

2) While waiting to be used in laboratory experiments animals are kept in solitary confinement in small cages. Alone and frightened they can hear the screams of the other animals being used.

3) Some of the animals used in laboratory experiments are pets which have been kidnapped, taken off the streets and sold to the vivisectors.

4) Animals used in experiments are blinded, burned, shot, injected and dissected. They have their eyes sewn up or their limbs broken. Chemicals are injected into their brains and their screams of anguish are coldly recorded.

5) Three quarters of the experiments performed by vivisectors are done without any anaesthetic.

6) Most vivisectors have no medical or veterinary training.

7) Scientists claim that animals are not sentient creatures and are incapable of suffering mental or physical pain.

8) All animals respond differently to threats of any kind depending on their circumstances (diet, cage size, etc.). None of these factors are allowed for by vivisectors. By locking an animal up in a cage experimenters have already invalidated their experiment because by altering the animal's surroundings the experimenter alters the animal's susceptibility, its habits, its instincts and its capacity to heal itself. Since these variations are not controlled (cages and surroundings differ) experiments performed on animals kept in cages are of no scientific value.

9) Many of the diseases which kill or cripple human beings do not affect any other members of the animal kingdom. It is, therefore, impossible to use different species to test drug therapies for these illnesses.

10) Doctors wouldn't test a drug intended for old people on children (or the other way round). So why test drugs intended for pregnant women on rats? No one would test a drug for premenstrual problems

on small boys and yet that would make far more sense than testing such a drug on male rats.

11) Drug tests done on animals can produce dangerously unreliable and misleading information. Thalidomide safely passed tests on animals. Penicillin and aspirin both kill cats. When Alexander Fleming discovered penicillin growing on a culture dish in 1928 he tested the drug on rabbits and discarded it when it seemed useless. Later the drug was tested on a cat and a human patient at the same time. The cat died and the human being lived. If doctors had relied upon animal experiments to decide whether or not penicillin was of any value the drug would have been discarded long ago. Penicillin even kills guinea pigs - the classic test animal for many drugs. Aspirin can be toxic to rats, mice, dogs, monkeys and guinea pigs as well as cats. Morphine sedates human beings but excites cats, goats and horses. Digitalis, one of the best established and most effective drugs for the treatment of heart disease, is so toxic to animals that if we had relied on animal tests it would have never been cleared for use by humans.

12) Vivisectors admit that most animal experiments are unreliable and produce results which are not relevant to human patients. But they don't know which experiments are unreliable. Logically, that means that all animal experiments are useless. If you don't know which experiments you can rely on, you can't rely on any of them.

13) The very unreliability and unpredictably of animal experiments is what makes them commercially valuable. Drug companies test on animals so that they can say that they have tested their drugs before marketing them. If the tests show that the drugs do not cause serious disorders when given to animals the companies say: 'There you are! We have tested our drug - and have proved it to be safe!' If, on the other hand, tests show that a drug does cause serious problems when given to animals the companies say: 'The animal experiments are, of course, unreliable and cannot be used to predict what will happen when the drug is given to humans. We have, however, tested our drug.' Tests which show that a drug causes cancer or some other serious disease when given to animals are ignored on the grounds that animals are different to people. However, tests which show that

a new drug doesn't kill animals are used as evidence that the drug is safe for human consumption. If you try a drug on enough different animals you can usually end up with at least one set of results which suggest that a drug is safe. Scores of drugs which cause cancer or other serious health problems in animals are widely prescribed for human patients. (See www.vernoncoleman.com for the names of 50).

14) Four out of ten patients who take a prescribed drug which has been tested for safety on animals can expect to suffer severe or noticeable side effects.

15) Surveys show that most practising doctors are opposed to vivisection on scientific grounds.

Appendix 2 Reasons For Being A Vegetarian

1) Avoiding meat is one of the best and simplest ways to cut down fat consumption. Modern farm animals are deliberately fattened up to increase profits. Eating fatty meat increases your chances of having a heart attack or developing cancer. The following diseases are known to be commoner among meat eaters: anaemia, appendicitis, arthritis, breast cancer, cancer of the colon, cancer of the prostate, constipation, diabetes, gallstones, gout, high blood pressure, indigestion, obesity, piles, strokes and varicose veins.

Lifelong vegetarians visit hospital 22% less often than meat eaters - and for shorter stays. Vegetarians have 20% lower blood cholesterol levels than meat eaters - and this reduces heart attack and cancer risks considerably.

2) Every minute of every working day thousands of animals are killed in slaughterhouses. Many animals are bled to death. Pain and misery are commonplace. In America alone 500,000 animals are killed for meat every hour.

3) The vast majority of cases of food poisoning are caused by eating meat.

4) Meat contains absolutely nothing - no proteins, vitamins or minerals - that the human body cannot obtain perfectly happily from a vegetarian diet.

5) African countries - where millions are starving to death - export grain to the developed world so that animals can be fattened for the dining tables of the affluent nations. This problem is getting worse now that agricultural land is widely used for growing crops to be used as a petrol and diesel substitute. If we ate the plants we grow - instead of feeding them to animals - the world's food shortage would disappear virtually overnight. One hundred acres of land will produce enough beef for 20 people but enough wheat to feed 240 people.

6) Food sold as `meat' can include the tail, head, feet, rectum and spinal cord of an animal. A sausage may contain ground up intestines. Who wants to eat the content of a pig's intestines?

7) Animals which are a year old are often far more rational - and capable of logical thought - than six week old babies. Pigs and sheep are far more intelligent than small children.

8) It's much easier to become - and stay - healthily slim if you are vegetarian. Vegetarians are fitter than meat eaters. Many of the world's most successful athletes are vegetarian.

9) Half the rainforests in the world have been destroyed to clear ground to graze cattle to make beefburgers. The burning of the forests contributes 20% of all greenhouse gases. Roughly 1,000 species a year become extinct because of the destruction of the rain forests. Around 300 million acres of American forest have been cleared to grow crops to feed cattle so that people can eat meat.

10) Approximately 60 million people a year die of starvation. All those lives could be saved if the starving people were allowed to eat just some of the grain used to fatten cattle and other farm animals. If Americans ate 10% less meat, world starvation would be a memory.

11) The world's fresh water shortage is being made worse by animal farming. And meat producers are the biggest polluters of water. It takes 2,500 gallons of water to produce one pound of meat.

12) Meat eaters consume hormones that were fed to the animals. No one knows what effect those hormones will have on human health. In some parts of the world as many as one in four hamburgers contains growth hormones that were originally given to cattle. Some farmers use tranquillisers to keep animals calm. Others routinely use antibiotics to stave off infection. When you eat meat you are eating those drugs. The indiscriminate feeding of antibiotics to animals is one of the main reasons for the rise in antibiotic resistant infections.

For more books by these authors please visit either the Amazon author page for Vernon Coleman or http://www.vernoncoleman.com/

Printed in Great Britain
by Amazon